Adventures in Canadian History

ATTACK ON MONTREAL

PIERRE BERTON

ATTACK ON MONTREAL

ILLUSTRATIONS BY PAUL MCCUSKER

An M&S Paperback from
McClelland & Stewart Inc.
The Canadian Publishers

An M&S Paperback Original from McClelland & Stewart Inc.
Copyright © 1995 by Pierre Berton Enterprises Ltd.

Canadian Cataloguing in Publication Data

Berton, Pierre, 1920-
    Attack on Montreal

(Adventures in Canadian history.   The battles of the War of 1812)
An M&S paperback original.
Includes index.
ISBN 0-7710-1419-8

1. Chateauguay, Battle of, Quebec, 1813 – Juvenile literature.*   2. Crysler's
Farm, Battle of, Ont., 1813 – Juvenile literature.*   3. Canada – History – War of
1812 – Campaigns – Juvenile literature.   I. Title.   II. Series: Berton, Pierre,
1920-   . Adventures in Canadian History. The battles of the War of 1812.

FC446.C5B4   1995   j971.0'34   C95-932039-3   E356.C5B4   1995

Series design by Tania Craan
Cover and text design by Stephen Kenny
Cover illustration by Scott Cameron
Interior illustrations by Paul McCusker
Maps by Geoffrey Matthews
Editor: Peter Carver

Typesetting by M&S, Toronto

Printed and bound in Canada

McClelland & Stewart Inc.
The Canadian Publishers
481 University Avenue
Toronto, Ontario
M5G 2E9

1 2 3 4 5   99 98 97 96 95

Contents

Maps appear on pages 16, 33, 39, 48, 60, and 61.

The events in this book actually happened as told here. Nothing has been made up. This is a work of non-fiction and there is archival evidence for every story and, indeed, every remark made in this book.

Adventures in Canadian History

Attack on Montreal

OVERVIEW
❧
The foolish war

O F ALL THE FOOLISH WARS fought in the nineteenth century, surely the silliest and most foolish was the American attempt to invade Canada between 1812 and 1814. The war was launched in order to give a black eye to the British, who were interfering with American ships trying to trade with French ports. The War of 1812, then, was simply a footnote to the Napoleonic Wars being fought on the European continent between England and France.

It was not only a foolish war, it was also a very strange one. Imagine a war in which everybody stopped fighting in the fall because the soldiers on both sides had to go home to get in the harvest!

In the winter it was just too cold to fight and in the spring many of the citizen soldiers had to work in the fields. So this war took place in the hot, lazy days of summer along the U.S.–Canadian border.

It was also a war fought by children, some of whom were as young as thirteen or fourteen. Many had not had a drink of hard liquor before joining up and so went into battle half-sozzled from their quarter-pint of whisky or tot of strong rum.

And it wasn't only the soldiers who were blind to what was happening. Half the time the generals didn't know what was going on. Where was the enemy? They didn't know, because communication was difficult and sometimes impossible. Neither the telephone nor radio had been invented.

Both sides used spies to find out how many fighting men were on the opposite side. Generally they got it wrong. The spies were mainly local farmers who couldn't always be trusted because this was also a civil war in which the people on both sides knew each other well.

For many, the border didn't exist. For years both Americans and Canadians had been smuggling goods across it.

The real enemy in this odd conflict was disease. On both sides, measles, typhus, typhoid, influenza, and dysentery probably put more men out of action than a bullet or a cannon ball. For this, the universal remedy was liquor. There were no wonder drugs, no real medicines.

The war along the St. Lawrence River was largely a war of musketry. The so-called Brown Bess musket was the basic infantry weapon, even though it was very inaccurate. The British troops and Canadian regulars were better with the musket because they were drilled to use it. They advanced in line, shoulder to shoulder, making no attempt to fire at individual targets. Instead they were taught to spray the enemy with a hail of bullets that wobbled down the unrifled barrels and might have flown anywhere.

That didn't matter. No enemy could withstand that wave of devastating lead. The forward line had been drilled to advance, to open fire on command, to drop to the ground and reload while the soldiers standing behind let go with a second volley. These tactics worked well in the open fields, such as Crysler's farm on the St. Lawrence. They were less effective in the forests, where the advance was held up by trees, stumps, and rough ground.

Under those conditions, the individualistic Americans preferred the long Tennessee rifle. It was far more accurate than the musket. Sharpshooters, hidden behind trees or folds in the ground, could take careful aim at enemy soldiers. That was how Isaac Brock, the general who led the British and Canadian forces at the Battle of Queenston Heights in 1812, was killed. A rifle bullet got him in the heart.

Brock was one of the few capable leaders in this crazy war. The American leadership was especially incompetent. They were not helped by the American volunteers, who had signed up for only a few months, and not for the duration, of the war. They could refuse to cross the border into a foreign country, a right protected by the U.S. constitution.

In many cases the Americans' hearts weren't in it. Why should they be? They weren't doing battle to save their nation as the Canadian regulars and volunteers were. Many of the people who lived along the border were new-comers to Canada. They had arrived after the American Revolution, because they were loyal to the British cause. For them this war would be one of the defining moments in the history of their raw, new nation. They knew that if they lost the war they could find themselves once again citizens of a land from which they had so recently fled. These people were Loyalists. They didn't want to be Americans, and they were prepared to fight to prevent it.

Canada is an independent nation today partly because of them.

CHAPTER ONE

The ailing general

O F ALL THE SILLY AND FOOLISH campaigns fought in this war, surely the silliest was the American attempt in the autumn of 1813 to sweep down the St. Lawrence River from Lake Ontario and seize Montreal.

The generals of the invading army were ageing incompetents, hated by their troops and despised by their fellow officers. They did not have the will to win – an essential in warfare. The malady of defeatism infected their followers, fourteen hundred of whom refused to cross the border to do battle. The men were sickly, badly fed and clothed, often untrained and ill equipped, and no match for their opponents.

The Americans outnumbered the defenders of Canada more than two to one but didn't know it; they were led to believe that they faced overwhelming odds and so, in effect, gave up in their minds before the battle was joined.

Major-General James Wilkinson, the officer in charge of the American invasion attempt, was a poor excuse for a soldier. He was a sick man, shivering with fever, so ill he had to be helped ashore when his troops reached the St. Lawrence.

Even if he'd been in the best of health, Wilkinson would have been an odd choice for commander-in-chief of the invading forces. He was getting on in years and almost universally despised. His entire career had been a catalogue of blunders, intrigues, investigations, plots, schemes, and deceptions.

Although he seemed pleasant enough on first encounter, he was unreliable, greedy for money, boastful, and dishonest. Three times he had been forced to resign from the army because of scandal.

He had once plotted against George Washington, then president of his country. He had even come close to treason when he had secret dealings with the Spanish. In spite of that, he had managed to rejoin the army and had risen to brigadier-general. Again he faced a court martial for conspiracy, treason, neglect of duty, and misuse of public money. But the court cleared him of the charges and he bounced back.

This was the man that the American high command had chosen to lead its newest attack. And so we find him in early October 1813, at Sackets Harbor not far from the point where the St. Lawrence River pours out of Lake Ontario.

The Americans had tried without success to capture the Niagara Peninsula and had been forced back to Fort George at the mouth of the Niagara River. Now they decided to change their plans. Their newest scheme was to cut the lifeline between Upper and Lower Canada. That would mean an all-out assault, either on Kingston or Montreal. If successful, Canada would effectively be cut in two. But neither the American secretary of war, John Armstrong, nor his ailing major-general, Wilkinson, could make up their minds which city to attack.

What a strange pair they made when they met at Sackets Harbor on October 13, 1813. The secretary was about to turn fifty-six, and he was handsome, aristocratic, and warlike. He and Wilkinson were once friends, but now he wanted Wilkinson's job.

The major-general was aware of Armstrong's ambitions but was too sick to care. He actually *wanted* to quit, but Armstrong wouldn't let him. "I would feed the old man with pap sooner than leave him behind," was the way he put it. In fact, the "old man" was scarcely a year older than Armstrong.

Armstrong himself was on shaky ground politically. U.S. President James Madison had no confidence in him. The secretary of state, James Monroe, was an enemy. Armstrong kept his job only through the support of powerful friends in New York.

Winter was approaching, but these two rivals couldn't agree on tactics. The secretary of war wanted to attack Kingston directly. Wilkinson dallied.

The two men kept contradicting one another. When Wilkinson insisted that Montreal was the target, Armstrong took the other side. Then both men changed positions until it became clear that neither expected that any attack on either stronghold could succeed. They had lost the battle in their minds before it began.

In war, one of the essentials for victory is confidence. All through history great military leaders have won out over heavy odds because they knew they could prevail. The will to win is as valuable as an extra cannon or a division of men.

In this case the Americans had three armies – one at Fort George on the Niagara would join with a second army at Sackets Harbor, while a third to the south on Lake Champlain would act in support.

By October 4, the two leading armies should have reached Grenadier Island at the mouth of the St. Lawrence, the jumping-off point for the final assault.

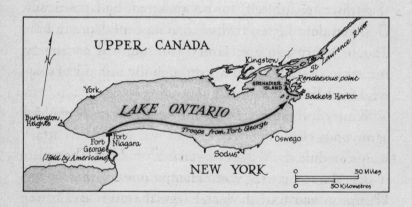

Lake Ontario, October 1813

But Wilkinson's troops were moving at a snail's pace. The contractor had figured it would take five days to load the boats. It actually took nineteen, throwing the schedule off-kilter. Worse, the ammunition and guns needed for the attack were loaded without any plan and scattered about the flotilla.

Hospital stores took priority over guns and powder. Hundreds of men lay ill because of the bad food and the wretched sanitation. The meat was rotten, the whisky polluted, the flour so bad that the medical officer said, "It would kill the best horse in Sackets Harbor." That September seven hundred officers and men lay ill. Within two months that number had doubled. The flotilla, when it did move, was a floating hospital, in the words of the camp surgeon.

The bread was the worst. It contained bits of soap, lime, and human excrement. And no wonder! The bakers took their water from a stagnant corner of the lake, no more than three feet (0.9 m) from the shore. The latrines were clustered only a few yards away. Naked men kneaded the dough. Nearby, in a cemetery, two hundred corpses lay buried in no more than a foot of sandy soil. The troops were weak from dysentery, but nothing was done for them. Wilkinson, who was supposed to be in charge, was as sick as anybody else.

Meanwhile, the supporting army from Lake Champlain under Major-General Wade Hampton was also delaying. Hampton had four thousand regular troops and fifteen hundred militia and he'd been ordered to support Wilkinson's attack. But Hampton hated Wilkinson so much he wouldn't take orders from him. As a result, when Wilkinson sent directions to Hampton two hundred miles (320 km) away, Hampton didn't even answer.

Hampton's army did make one attack on September 21, which failed because the weather was so hot. His horses and men were so desperate with thirst that they had to retreat and march seventy miles (112 km) back to their present spot, Four Corners on the Châteauguay River.

Armstrong – the only man who could talk to Hampton – told him to hold fast. "Keep up the enemy's doubts, with regard to the real point of your attack." The fact was, however, that Armstrong himself didn't know where the real point of attack would be.

At last, on October 16, he told Hampton to move down the Châteauguay River and cross the Canadian border. There he would be able to support a thrust against Kingston. Or, if Montreal were chosen, he could wait until the main body headed down the St. Lawrence.

By mid-October only half of the combined forces had reached the rendezvous point on Grenadier Island. A winter storm had been raging for a week, lashing the waters of the lake with rain, snow, and hail. The few boats that did set off were destroyed or forced back to the harbour. By October 19, when the storm subsided, the main body set off for Grenadier Island. The ground was now thick with snow, but no one had yet decided whether Kingston or Montreal would be the main point of the attack. Did these American generals really believe they could seize Canada before winter?

L ET US NOW LOOK IN ON TWO Canadian farmers, Jacob Manning and his brother, David, who had been held prisoner by the Americans in a log stable on Benjamin Roberts's farm, near Châteauguay Four Corners, New York State. That is where Wade Hampton's army was camped. On October 21, 1813, the two farmers learned that Hampton wanted to talk to them.

The brothers were spies – part of a group recruited by the British from the settlers of the townships north of the border. This was smugglers' country, where everybody knew everybody else, and where everybody was involved in spiriting goods illegally across the border. The Americans sneaked barrels of potash into Canada for sale in Montreal. The Canadians slipped over the imaginary line pulling hand sleds loaded with ten-gallon (45-L) kegs of whisky. Everyone knew about it. How could you hide the tell-tale signs? So much beef was smuggled into Canada for the British army that herds of cattle had left tracks in the woods along the frontier.

The Mannings, who had been supplying the British army with reports of the American troop movements, had been surprised in their sleep on October 2. Since then they had been held under suspicion. Now they were brought under guard to Hampton's headquarters in a tavern.

Hampton was well known for his impatience, arrogance, and bad temper. A self-made man, with all the stubborn pride of that species, he was difficult to get along with. An uneducated farm boy, orphaned early in life by an Indian raid, he was well on his way to becoming the wealthiest planter in the United States. He had a greed for land and had made his fortune in speculation, much of it shady. He owned vast plantations in South Carolina, with thousands of slaves, some of whom he had brought along on this campaign.

He had been a good politician and a good soldier during the American Revolution, but now he was in his sixtieth year and had lost much of his drive. He was so unpopular that some officers had refused to serve under him. Some, in fact, had threatened to quit the army if Hampton were placed in charge of the Niagara frontier.

His task was to cross the border and march down the Châteauguay River to the point where it joined the St. Lawrence near Montreal. The Americans thought that an attack on Kingston would confuse the British. Alternatively, Hampton's army was ready to join Wilkinson on his sweep to Montreal.

Neither side knew the other's strength. Hampton had

no idea how many men the British and Canadians had. The British were just as much in the dark about the American strength and strategy. That's why Hampton had called on the Mannings. He wanted David Manning to take his fastest horse, gallop to Montreal, and bring back information about the size of the British defence force stationed there.

But when he offered Manning a handsome reward, Manning turned him down.

"Are you not an American?" Hampton demanded.

"Yes," said Manning. "I was born on the American side and I have many relations, but I am true to the British flag."

He was, in fact, a United Empire Loyalist – one of the "Tories" (as they were called) who refused to fight against the British during the American Revolution and who were forced to move north of the border.

At this response, Hampton's famous temper flared up. He told the Manning brothers they were in his power. If they didn't toe the line, he would send them to the military prison.

That didn't frighten the two backwoodsmen. They replied, boldly, that anything would be better than being held in a filthy stable. So Hampton tried to squeeze more information from them. Was there a fort in Montreal? They told him that there wasn't, but he refused to believe it.

He took the two men to the tavern window overlooking a farm and proudly pointed out the size of his army. Spread

Hampton confronts the Mannings.

out before them the brothers saw an imposing spectacle: thousands of men striking their tents, cavalry cantering about, the infantry drilling in platoons. It was clear that Hampton was about to move his army across the border into Canada.

The general now asked how far the Mannings thought a force of that size could go. Jacob Manning couldn't resist a cheeky answer: "If it has good luck, it may get to Halifax," he said, for Halifax was where all prisoners of war were sent.

That infuriated Hampton, who told his officer of the guard, a local militiaman named Hollenbeck, to take the brothers back to their stable prison and to keep them there for three days so that they couldn't get word of his advance to the British.

But Hollenbeck was an old friend and neighbour, and once they were out of Hampton's earshot, he asked, "Do you want anything to eat?"

"No," said Jacob.

"Well, then, put for home," said Hollenbeck, and off the Mannings went to warn the British of the American advance.

CHAPTER THREE

∾
The "Marquis of cannon powder"

THE MANNINGS WEREN'T the only ones to warn of the American advance. Hampton's troops crossed the border and reached Spears's farm at the junction of the Châteauguay and Outarde rivers on October 21. There they routed members of a small band of Canadian soldiers who escaped and sounded the alarm.

People living near the border had been in a state of tension for weeks, not knowing exactly where the Americans would attack. Now it was obvious that Hampton would advance along the cart track that bordered the Châteauguay. His object was the St. Lawrence, and surely Montreal.

In the coming battle the defence of Canada would fall almost entirely on the French Canadian militia – citizen soldiers who supported the regular forces. More than three hundred were moving up the river road to a meeting place in the hardwood forest not far from the future settlement of Allan's Corners. Few had uniforms. Many wore homespun blouses and blue toques. Two flank companies of the notorious Devil's Own battalion wore green coats with red facings. These men had been recruited from the slums of Montreal and Quebec. The battalion got its name because of its reputation for thievery and disorder.

The following morning a more reliable force arrived. These were the Canadian Fencibles and Voltigeurs. The latter unit consisted not of habitants but of voyageurs, lumbermen, and city-bred youths. They had been drilled like regulars all that winter by their leader, a thirty-five-year-old career soldier, Lieutenant-Colonel Charles-Michel d'Irumberry de Salaberry. They wore smart grey uniforms and fur hats and were so tough that they thought nothing of fighting in their bare feet.

De Salaberry would emerge from this battle as an authentic Canadian hero. He was short in stature, big-chested, and muscular. He was a strict disciplinarian – brusque, impetuous, often harsh with his men. He had been a soldier since the age of fourteen, and three younger brothers had already died in service. His father's patron and his own was the Duke of Kent, the father of Queen Victoria.

A superior called him "my dear Marquis of cannon powder," but his Voltigeurs admired him because he was fair-minded, and they sang about him:

This is our major,
The embodiment of the devil
Who gives us death.

There is no wolf or tiger
Who could be so rough;
Under the openness of the sky
There is not his equal.

His men knew the story of the scar on de Salaberry's brow. That went back to his days in the West Indies when an arrogant German killed his best friend in duel.

"I come just now from dispatching a French Canadian into another world," the duellist boasted.

De Salaberry replied, "We are going to finish lunch and then you will have the pleasure of dispatching another."

But it was the German who was dispatched and de Salaberry merely scarred.

For weeks he had been spying on Hampton's pickets at Châteauguay Four Corners. Now he prepared to meet the full force not far from the point where the Châteauguay meets the English River.

He had chosen his position with care. Half a dozen ravines cut their way through the sandy soil at right angles to the Châteauguay River. These would be his main line of defence. The first three lines were only two hundred yards (180 m) apart, the fourth lay half a mile (792 m) to the rear. Two more lay some distance downriver near La Fourche, where the reserve army and headquarters would be stationed, six lines of fighting men, giving his army depth.

By noon on October 22, de Salaberry and his axemen had hacked down scores of trees, whose tangled branches formed a breastwork on the forward lip of each ravine. A mile (2 km) in front of the forward ravine, on Robert Bryson's farm, de Salaberry found a coulee, forty feet (12 m) deep . Here his men built another obstacle, or abatis, extending in a half-circle from the deep gorge on the left to a swamp in the forest on their right. It would be hard for the Americans to get around these obstacles and attack from the flanks. To hit at the Canadians, they would have to mount a frontal attack – always a difficult and dangerous tactic against a stubborn enemy.

They were still hacking down trees and piling up slash when an unexpected reinforcement arrived. This was the battalion of the Select Embodied Militia, a mixed bag of French Canadians and Scottish farmers who had arrived at top speed. Their commander, Lieutenant-Colonel "Red George" Macdonell, was used to quick action. When he had been asked how soon he could get under way, he had responded briskly, "As soon as my men have done dinner." The battalion made the exhausting trip in just sixty hours, without a man missing.

That same day, October 24, Hampton's main body moved deeper into Canada along a road his engineers had hacked through the bush. A spy watched them go by, carefully counted the guns, the wagons, and the troops, and immediately sent a detailed report to the British.

The spy also reported cheering news: more than fourteen hundred American militiamen had bluntly refused to cross the border and invade Canada in this silly war. That

De Salaberry's men build the abatis.

was their right under the American constitution. No citizen soldier was required to fight on foreign soil if he didn't want to. Only regular army men were required to.

As a result Hampton's army was badly depleted. In addition, his men were poorly clothed; in fact, they had so little winter gear that they had to gamble to get greatcoats. Nor were the Southerners – mostly from Virginia – used to the Canadian weather. One regiment of a thousand had already lost half its force due to sickness.

Meanwhile, Hampton learned the main attack would be on Montreal. Wilkinson was bringing his army down the St. Lawrence by boat and would join Hampton for the assault on the city. The idea of attacking Kingston was abandoned.

By this time the British were aware of the full American strategy. De Salaberry was badly outnumbered in spite of American afflictions and illness. Hampton had assembled about four thousand men at Spears's farm. All that stood between his army and the St. Lawrence River were the sixteen hundred militiamen seven miles (11 km) downriver.

The Canadian Voltigeurs and Fencibles would bear the brunt of the attack in the forward ravine. They would wait behind a tangle of roots and branches, knowing they were heavily outgunned and that the odds against them were better than two to one. The spy had counted nine cannons, plus a Howitzer and a mortar. And he believed that more were moving down towards the Canadian lines by another route.

Who was the spy who seemed to know everything that was going on? He was, of course, David Manning, the Loyalist farmer whom Hampton believed to be safely behind bars. But Hampton hadn't reckoned with the uncertain loyalties of the border people. He didn't know and would never know that Hollenbeck, his sergeant of the guard, was not only David Manning's friend and neighbour but also an informant himself. Hollenbeck was perfectly prepared to salute the American flag in public, while secretly supplying the British with all the information and gossip they would need.

Chapter Four

The battle of Châteauguay

MAJOR-GENERAL WADE HAMPTON realized he could not storm around the flank of the French Canadians and try to take them in the rear. Their position was anchored between gorge and swamp. He ordered Robert Purdy, colonel of the veteran U.S. 4th Infantry, to take fifteen hundred crack troops and ford the Châteauguay River at its lowest point and proceed along the opposite bank under cover of darkness.

Hampton hoped that, in this roundabout way, they would get around de Salaberry's defences on the opposite shore. At dawn they would recross the river by way of a second ford and attack the enemy from behind their lines. As soon as Hampton heard gunfire from Purdy, he would launch a frontal attack on the barrier of trunks and branches. In this way, he thought, de Salaberry would be caught between the claws of a pincer.

It looked good on paper, but it was impossible to carry out in reality. Here was Hampton proposing that Purdy and his men would plunge through sixteen miles (26 km) of a thick wood and hemlock swamp in the pitch dark. That would be difficult for anybody who knew his way around. For strangers it would be a nightmare.

The guides they took with them were worthless. In fact, they told Hampton that they didn't know the country. But Hampton was so stubbornly sure of his plan that he paid no attention. Nothing could change his mind.

The result was disaster. Hampton went along with the expedition to the first ford of the river, then returned to camp. It was a cold night. Rain began to fall. There was no

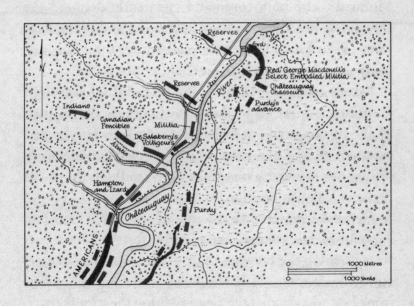

The Battle of Châteauguay, Phase I

moon. On the far side of the river, Purdy's men floundered in a creek, stumbled into a swamp, tripped over fallen trees, and staggered through thick piles of underbrush. All order vanished.

After two miles (3 km) the guides, too, were lost. Purdy realized he couldn't go on in the dark. And so his men spent the night in the rain, shivering in their summer clothing, not even able to light a fire for fear of being discovered.

Back at camp, Hampton received a rude shock. A letter from Washington instructed him to build huts for winter quarters right there at Four Corners, south of the border. Hampton was flabbergasted. Winter quarters at Four Corners? He had expected to spend the winter at Montreal! The high command apparently doubted the expedition would ever reach its objective, and so the fight went out of him. He tried to recall Purdy's force but realized that in that black night it could not be found.

Dawn arrived, wan and damp, the dead leaves of autumn drooping from the trees. Purdy shook his men awake in the tangle of brush and swamp where he had camped. Across the river the Americans were already setting out to move along the wagon road that led to the French Canadian position.

De Salaberry was not expecting an attack that morning. A party of his axemen, guarded by forty soldiers, was strengthening the bulwark in front of the forward ravine. Suddenly, at ten o'clock – surprise! – the first Americans came bounding across the clearing firing their muskets.

De Salaberry was well to the rear when he heard the staccato sound of gunfire. He moved up quickly with reinforcements. The workmen had already scattered, and the Americans, cheering wildly, were pushing forward, only to be halted by Canadian musket fire.

De Salaberry, a commanding figure in his grey fur-trimmed coat, moved to the top of the abatis. He climbed up on a large hemlock that had been uprooted by the wind. There, hidden from the enemy by two large trees, he watched the blue line of Americans move down the river towards him.

But the firing had sputtered out, and the expected attack did not come because Hampton was waiting to hear from Purdy across the river. His men settled down to cook lunch. On the Canadian side of the bulwark a company of French Canadian militia knelt in prayer and were told by their captain that, having done their duty to their God, he now expected they would do their duty to their king.

Meanwhile, de Salaberry's scouts had found a few stragglers emerging from the dense woods along the far bank of the river, revealing Purdy's presence. Purdy was badly behind schedule. His force of fifteen hundred men had not gone far enough. In fact, at this point they were directly across from de Salaberry's forward position.

On the Canadian side, word got back to Red George Macdonell, who had been given the task of guarding the ford in the rear. Macdonell sent two of his companies across the river to reinforce a small band of Châteauguay

Chasseurs – untrained local farmers conscripted into the militia for Canada.

Macdonell's men moved through the dense pine forest, peering through the tangle of naked trunks, looking for the advancing Americans. Purdy's advance guard – about a hundred men – were splashing through a cedar swamp when the two forces met. Both sides opened fire.

A scene of confusion followed. Macdonell's men stood fast, but the untrained Chasseurs turned and fled. The American advance party also turned tail and plunged back through the woods. There, Purdy's main body, thinking they were Canadians, opened fire and killed some of their own men.

Purdy thought the woods were full of enemies. He tried to regroup his men and sent a message to Hampton asking for help. The courier headed for Spears's farm, only to discover that Hampton had left and had moved upriver. At this point Hampton had no idea whether or not Purdy had achieved his objective. He couldn't tell what was happening on the far bank because the forest was so thick.

At two that afternoon Hampton finally decided to act. He ordered Brigadier-General George Izard to attack in line. Izard, another South Carolina aristocrat, was a competent professional soldier. His well-drilled brigade moved down the road towards the vast tangle of the Canadian abatis.

Behind that breastwork, de Salaberry's men watched the tall American officer ride forward. Afterward, some remembered his cry: "Brave Canadians, surrender your-selves; we wish you no harm!"

In response de Salaberry himself fired. The American fell from his horse and the battle was joined.

Badly outnumbered, de Salaberry now depended on a series of deceptions to fool the Americans into believing they were facing a superior force. He called to his bugler to sound the call to open fire. The noise of exploding muskets mingled with the cries of a small body of Caughnawaga Indians hidden in the woods to the right of the Canadian line. The Americans, firing by platoons, as if on a parade ground, poured volley after volley into the woods, believing the main Canadian force was hidden there. But the lead balls whistled harmlessly through the treetops.

Now Red George Macdonell sounded his own bugles as a signal that he was advancing. Other bugles took up the refrain. De Salaberry sent buglers into the woods to trumpet in every direction. As a result the Americans thought they were heavily outnumbered.

Izard hesitated. Finally some of Macdonell's men appeared at the edge of the woods wearing red coats. They popped back into the woods, turned their jackets inside out (because they were lined with white flannel), and popped out again. The Americans thought they were a different corps.

Twenty Indians were sent to dash through the woods to the right of the Canadian line, appearing from time to time, brandishing tomahawks. The Americans, unable to tell one Indian from another, and seeing them popping in and out, thought there were hundreds of them working in the depths.

"Defy, my damned ones!" cried de Salaberry. "Defy! If you do not dare, you are not men!"

The battle continued for an hour. The Americans fired rolling volleys, platoon by platoon. The Canadians returned the fire raggedly. There were few casualties on either sides. The Americans didn't attempt to storm the barrier.

Now de Salaberry focused his attention on the far side of the river. The two Canadian companies that had driven off Purdy's forward troops were moving cautiously towards the colonel's position and tangling with his main force.

De Salaberry hurried to the bank of the river, clambered up a tree, and began to shout orders in French so the Americans couldn't understand him. He lined up his forces along with the Indians and militia to fire on Purdy's men if they emerged from the woods.

The two forces faced each other in the swampy forest. Captain Charles Daly of the Embodied Militia ordered his men to kneel before they fired. That manoeuvre saved their lives. Purdy's overwhelming body of crack troops responded with a shattering volley but most of it passed harmlessly over the Canadians' heads.

Now Purdy's men swept forward on the river flank of the Canadians, determined to take them from the rear. The situation was critical. But as the Americans burst out of the woods and onto the river bank, de Salaberry, watching through his glass, gave the order to fire. The bushes on the far side erupted into a sheet of flame. The Americans, badly mangled, fled into the forest. Exhausted by fourteen hours of struggle, they could fight no longer.

A lull followed. Hampton, astride his horse on the right of his troops, wasn't sure what to do. A courier had just swum the river to tell him about Purdy's predicament. That rattled the major-general.

He considered his next move. Izard hadn't tried to storm the barrier; that would cause heavy casualties. De Salaberry's ruses had fooled Hampton. The American

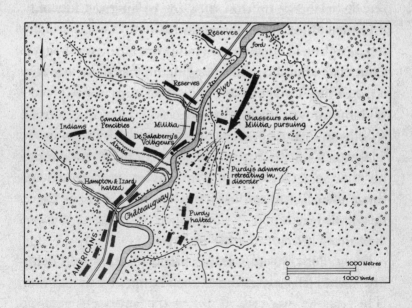

The Battle of Châteauguay, Phase II

general thought there were at least five or six thousand men opposing him, although there were only a few hundred. De Salaberry had at most three hundred men in his advanced position. Macdonell had about two hundred in reserve. The remainder were several miles to the rear at La Fourche, where the English River joined the Châteauguay. There were only six hundred of these and none were in the fight.

De Salaberry's boldness and Hampton's failure of nerve decided the outcome of the Battle of Châteauguay. Compared to other battles in this foolish war, it was really no more than a skirmish, with men on both sides peppering away at each other at long range with little effect. In fact, de Salaberry, on the other side of the river, lost only three men killed and eight wounded.

The fight had gone out of Hampton. Purdy was bogged down. The afternoon was dragging on and there was rain in the offing. Twilight was only a few hours away.

Hampton was dogged by indecision. He was jealous of Wilkinson, who he knew would gain all the glory if Hampton won the battle. He was furious at Armstrong, the U.S. secretary of war, who was resigned to defeat. Above all he lacked confidence in himself. He did not have the will to win.

Most of his force hadn't even got into the battle. He hadn't used his big guns. Izard's brigade had stopped fighting. And so Major-General Wade Hampton sent an order to Purdy to break off the engagement of the right bank and told his bugler to sound the withdrawal.

The Canadians watched in astonishment as Hampton's brigade retreated in perfect order. They made no attempt to harass it, waiting instead for the rally that never came. De Salaberry expected a renewed attack at any moment. He sent back word to all the houses along the river to prepare for a retreat and to burn all the buildings. It wasn't necessary.

Colonel Purdy, hidden in the forest, knew nothing of this. As the sun set he started to move his wounded across the river on rafts. He sent a message to Hampton asking that a regiment be detached to cover his landing. He was shocked and angered to learn that Hampton had already retreated three miles (5 km), deserting him without support.

The next morning the once elite detachment struggled into Hampton's camp. Many had no hats, knapsacks, or weapons. Their clothing was torn, they were half-starved and sick with fatigue. Their morale was shattered.

Purdy was thoroughly disgusted. Several of his officers had behaved badly in the skirmish. But when Purdy tried to arrest them for desertion or cowardice, Hampton countermanded the orders.

Purdy reported that somebody in the commissary was selling the troops' rations, but Hampton brushed that away. In Purdy's view the sick were so badly neglected that many had died from lack of medical care. He was convinced that Hampton was drinking so heavily that he was no longer able to command.

Meanwhile, de Salaberry felt that he was being snubbed by the British high command. The French Canadian militia had borne the brunt of the battle. One thousand fresh troops were available to harass the enemy and de Salaberry wanted to commit them, but his senior commanders wouldn't allow it. De Salaberry was embittered because he believed he had not been given the sole credit for repulsing the American invasion. Sir George Prevost, the Governor General of Canada, wanted his share of glory.

Hampton, meanwhile, ordered his entire force back across the border to Four Corners "for the preservation of the army," a statement that would astonish the British, who were convinced that the Americans were planning a second attack. On October 28, Indian scouts confirmed that Hampton was retiring.

De Salaberry called the battle "a most extraordinary affair," and so it was: 460 troops had forced the retreat of 4,000. The victors had lost only five killed, and sixteen wounded, with four men missing. The Americans lost fifty.

It was a small battle, but for Canada it was profoundly significant. A handful of civilian soldiers, almost all French Canadians, with scarcely any help managed to turn back the gravest invasion threat of the war. If Hampton had reached the St. Lawrence to join with Wilkinson's advancing army,

Montreal would likely have fallen. With Montreal gone and Upper Canada cut off, the British presence in North America would be reduced to a narrow strip in Quebec. Although the Battle of Châteauguay looks like no more than a silly skirmish, without that victory Canada could not have stretched from sea to sea.

CHAPTER FIVE

~

"Damn, such an army!"

O N GRENADIER ISLAND IN the St. Lawrence, James
Wilkinson realized, as he wrote the secretary of war,
"all our hopes have been very nearly blasted." Here, on the
first of November, the great flotilla designed to conquer
Montreal was stuck. The troops were drenched from the
incessant rain. Boats were smashed, stores scattered, hundreds sick, scores drunk.

Wilkinson, of course, had to put the best face on these
disasters. He relied on God to solve his problems:

"Thanks to the same Providence which placed us in
jeopardy, we are surmounting our difficulties and, God
willing, I shall pass Prescott on the night of the 1st or 2nd
proximo, if some unforeseen obstacle does not present to
forbid me."

But there were plenty of unforeseen obstacles. On the
journey from Sackets Harbor to Grenadier Island – a mere
eighteen miles (29 km) – the American flotilla had been
scattered by gales so furious that great trees were uprooted
on the shores. Some boats hadn't even arrived.

A third of all the rations had been lost. It was impossible to disentangle the rest from the other equipment. Shivering in the driving rain, some of the men had torn oilcloths off the ration boxes for protection, so the bread became soggy and inedible. Hospital stores were pilfered; hogsheads of brandy and port wine, which the doctors believed essential for good health, were tapped and consumed. The guard was drunk, and the officer in charge found he couldn't keep his men sober.

The boats were badly overloaded. They became difficult to row or steer. Sickness increased daily. One hundred and ninety-six men were so ill that they had to be sent back to Sackets Harbor. Wilkinson himself was flat on his back with dysentery.

In spite of the meagre food, the American islanders preferred to sell their produce to the British on the north shore. One fourteen-year-old drummer boy, Jarvis Hanks, tried to buy some potatoes from a local farmer for fifty cents a bushel. The man refused. He said he could get a dollar a bushel in Kingston. So that night Hanks and his friends stole the entire crop.

Some of the officers still half-believed that Wilkinson intended to attack at Kingston and not Montreal at all. It wasn't until October 30 that Wilkinson made up his mind to join with Hampton and head for the French Canadian capital.

The head of the American fleet, Commodore Isaac Chauncey, was "disappointed and mortified" when he heard that. He didn't believe the plan had much chance of success with the winter coming on.

Finally the troops set out down the St. Lawrence. Three brigades headed for the next rendezvous point at French Creek on the American side of the river directly opposite Gananoque. One made it; the weather forced the other two back.

The American flotilla is scattered by the storm.

The bulk of the army arrived on November 3, but Wilkinson was now so ill he had to be carried ashore. Meanwhile British gunboats skirmished with the Americans, which delayed the assault still further. The full flotilla didn't reach French Creek until November 5.

The valley of the St. Lawrence was bathed in an Indian summer glow. Six thousand men in 350 boats formed a

procession five miles (8 km) long to slide down the great river with flags flying and brass buttons gleaming, fifes and drums playing, and boatmen singing. There was only one drawback: British gunboats were not far behind.

By November 6, the flotilla reached Morristown, four days late. Wilkinson had to halt now because he feared the British guns at Prescott, a dozen miles (19 km) downstream. He decided to strip his boats of all armament, march his men along the river bank, hauling the supplies in wagons, and pass Prescott with the lightly manned boats under cover of darkness. That would delay him another day.

While the boats were being unloaded and the troops formed, he issued a proclamation to the British settlers along the river, urging the farmers to stay home, promising that persons and property of those who didn't fight would be protected.

Wilkinson Moves on Montreal, October -November 1813

He might as well have been talking to the wind. For this was Loyalist country. The settlers were already priming their muskets to harass the American flotilla. The river shortly became a shooting gallery, with gunfire exploding from the bushes at every twist of the channel.

At noon, Wilkinson learned of the defeat at Châteauguay. He was told that "our best troops behaved in the most rascally manner."

"Damn such an army!" Wilkinson cried. "A man might as well be in hell as command it."

However, with Hampton's forces intact, the two armies numbered close to eleven thousand men. Surely that would be enough to seize Montreal?

At eight that night, with the river shrouded in a heavy fog, the flotilla began to move out into the water with muffled oars. The fog lifted and the leading boat was subjected to a fearful cannonade. Fifty twenty-four-pound

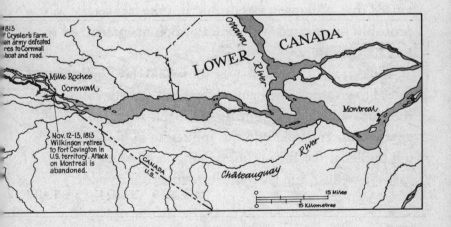

(11-kg) balls were hurled at her from the Canadian shore but with no effect, because the guns were out of range and set too high to do any damage.

The flotilla halted and waited for the moon to set. Its pale light, gleaming on the bayonets of the troops trudging along the shore, had helped to identify the manoeuvre to the British, as had signal lights flashed in the homes of certain Ogdensburg citizens friendly to the British cause.

In the midst of this uproar, Colonel Winfield Scott arrived. Wilkinson had left him in charge of a skeleton command at Fort George on the Niagara frontier until relieved by New York State militia. Now he had ridden for thirty hours through the forests of northern New York in a sleet storm.

Taken aboard Wilkinson's passage boat, Scott felt stimulated by the bursting of shells and rockets. He found it sublime though he distrusted and despised his general, whom he called an "unprincipled imbecile." He was convinced that Wilkinson was drunk. But the fact was he was probably intoxicated with doses of opium, prescribed to ease his dysentery.

Wilkinson's condition was so serious he finally was forced to go ashore. Benjamin Forsyth of the rifle company met him and helped him up the bank with the aid of another officer. Wilkinson was muttering to himself, hurling insults at the British, threatening to blow the enemy's garrison to dust, and lay waste the entire countryside.

The two officers sat him down by the hearth, posted a guard at the door to keep the spectacle from prying eyes, and tried to decide what to do. By this time Wilkinson was singing bawdy songs and telling obscene stories, until he began to nod, and to the relief of all, allowed himself to be put to bed.

November 7 dawned bright and clear, a perfect day for sailing. But the British had reinforced every bend with cannon and sharpshooters. Wilkinson detached an elite corps of twelve hundred soldiers to clear the bank, with Forsyth's riflemen detailed as rearguard. By nightfall the flotilla had only moved eight miles (13 km).

Wilkinson was now losing his nerve as Wade Hampton had before him. In his weakened condition he believed himself to be in the grip of forces he could not control. He had little faith in his own army. He knew that he had been held up too long, giving the British a chance to catch him from the rear. Already the word was that two army schooners and seven gunboats had reached Prescott, carrying at least a thousand men.

In his fevered imagination, the general magnified the forces opposed to him. The farmers on the Canadian shore had purposely been stuffing the heads of their American interrogators with wild stories about the dangers ahead. They described terrifying rapids, batteries of guns at every narrows, savage Indians prowling the forest, and no fodder for the horses. It was said that the army would face five thousand British regulars and twenty thousand Canadian militia. That was a fantastic overstatement, but it fooled the doddering major-general.

On the following day, Wilkinson, who could hardly get out of his bunk, called a council of war. It was finally agreed to carry on to Montreal. He was still concerned about the forces on the Canadian side. He ordered one of his commanders, Jacob Brown, to disembark his brigade and take command of the combined forces clearing the Canadian shore.

Ahead lay the dreaded Long Sault rapids, eight miles (13 km) of white water in which no boat could manoeuvre under enemy fire. Brown's job was to clear the banks so the flotilla could make it through the rapids without fear of attack. With the British at his rear, Wilkinson couldn't get under way until Brown reached the head of the rapids. Wilkinson moved eleven miles (18 km), but with the British nipping at his heels he stopped again.

On November 10, the British gunboats moved in to the attack at the same time. Brown's force on the shore ran into heavy resistance. By the time he'd cleared the bank, the pilots refused to take the boat through the white water.

The American flotilla moved two miles (3 km) past John Crysler's farm to Cook's Point, a mile or two (2 or 3 km) above the rapids. The troops built fires on the shore, tearing off the farmers' rail fences. All night they shivered in the rain and sleet. Jarvis Hanks, the drummer boy in the 11th, pulled a leather cap over his head and curled up so close to the fire that by morning both his cap and his shoes were charred.

Meanwhile, Brown had gone aboard Wilkinson's boat to find exactly who was in charge. But Wilkinson was too sick to see him. It had taken eight days for the fleet to move eighty miles (128 km). A log drifting down the river could make the same distance in two.

CHAPTER SIX

The battle of Crysler's farm

IT WOULD BE PLEASANT TO be able to visit the scene of one of the great British–Canadian victories on the shores of the St. Lawrence and follow the tactics of the troops that day. Alas, John Crysler's farm is no more. The broad field where the battle took place is under water, part of the St. Lawrence Seaway. Before the area was flooded, soil was dug from the site and a mound constructed not far away on which a monument was placed to record the battle. About one kilometre distant, Upper Canada Village stands – a collection of venerable houses moved from the seaway site to give some idea of the way people lived during the early days of the nineteenth century.

On November 11, 1813, dawn broke, bleak and soggy. John Loucks, a militiaman and one of the three troopers in the Provincial Dragoons posted with three companies of the Canadian Voltigeurs and a few Indians a mile ahead of the main British force, spotted a movement through the trees ahead. A party of Americans was advancing from Cook's Point, where the American flotilla was anchored. A musket exploded in the woods on Loucks's left, where a party of Indians was stationed. The Americans replied with a volley that kicked sand in front of the troopers' horses. Young Loucks drove off at a gallop to warn the British commander, Lieutenant-Colonel Joseph Wanton Morrison.

As the troopers dashed through the ranks of the 49th Regiment, Lieutenant John Sewell was toasting a piece of breakfast pork on the point of his sword. He needed the hot nourishment because he had slept on the cold ground all night with his gun between his legs to protect it from the icy rain. Now he realized there would be no time for breakfast as his company commander shouted, "Jack, drop cooking, the enemy is advancing."

The British scrambled into position behind a stout rail fence, but the warning was far too early. All that Loucks had seen was an American scouting party.

Back at his headquarters in the Crysler farmhouse, Morrison assessed his position. He had been chasing Wilkinson and the gunboats for five days, ever since word had reached Kingston that the American attack would be on Montreal. Finally he had caught up with him. Would the Americans stand and fight? Or would the chase continue? With a force of only eight hundred men to challenge Wilkinson's seven thousand, Morrison wasn't eager for a pitched battle.

However, he realized if he did have a battle, it would be on ground of his own choosing. It would be a European-style battle on an open plain where his men could manoeuvre as on a parade ground, standing shoulder to shoulder in parallel lines, each man occupying twenty-two inches (55 cm) of space, advancing with a bayonet, wheeling easily when ordered, or into a staggered series of platoons, each one supporting its neighbour.

This was the kind of warfare for which his two regiments had been trained – the Green Tigers, known for the fierceness of their attack, and his own regiment, the 89th. Morrison was an old soldier who had learned his trade well. Like his father before him, he had served half his life in the British army, shifting from continent to continent whenever his country called him.

He understood battle tactics. He had chosen his position carefully, anchoring his thin line between the river on his right, where the gunboats would give him support, and a black ash swamp about half a mile (792 m) to his left, which nobody could penetrate. His men were protected by a heavy fence of cedar logs five feet (1.5 m) high. Ahead for half a mile (792 m) a muddy field stretched, covered with winter wheat, cut with gullies, and bisected by a stream that trickled out of the swamp to become a deep ravine running into the St. Lawrence.

Behind the fence on the right was the 49th, close to the river and to the King's Highway that ran along the bank. On the left was the 89th. Its soldiers wore the scarlet, but the battle-seasoned 49th hid its distinctive green tunics under grey overcoats.

Half a mile (792 m) forward of this were light troops, including the Canadian Fencibles. Another half-mile (792 m) farther on, the skirmishers – Indians and Voltigeurs, the latter almost invisible in their grey home-spun, were concealed behind rocks, stumps, and fences.

Morrison was heavily outnumbered. But he counted the ability of his troops to hold fast against the more in-dividualistic Americans. It was here that the contrast between the two countries became apparent.

Wilkinson's men were experienced bush fighters. They were brought up with firearms and blooded in frontier Indian wars. They were used to taking individual action in skirmishes where each man would have to act on his own if he was to escape with a whole skin.

On the other hand, the British soldier was drilled to stand unflinchingly with his comrades in the face of exploding cannon, to hold his fire until ordered so that the maximum effect of the spraying muskets could be felt, and then to move in machinelike unison with hundreds of others, each man an automaton.

The British regulars followed orders implicitly. The Americans were less obedient, sometimes to the point of anarchy.

Morrison had one advantage, though he didn't know it. The American high command had collapsed. The chief of the invading army and his second-in-command both lay deathly ill, unable to direct any battle.

Wilkinson's deputy, Morgan Lewis, was dosing himself on blackberry jelly, but he was even less capable than his superior. Wilkinson couldn't get out of his bunk. He waited to hear from Jacob Brown on shore that the rapids ahead had been cleared of British troops.

At half past ten, a dragoon arrived to tell him the rapids were clear. But the commander-in-chief was in a quandary. The British gunboats were just behind him: What if they should just slip past?

He gave an order for the flotilla to get under way and told Brigadier-General John Boyd, on land, to begin marching his men towards Cornwall below the rapids. But even as he did that he was alerted to the presence of the British on Crysler's field. At the same time, the British gunboats began to lob shot in his direction. So Wilkinson held up and decided to try to destroy the small British force before moving on.

Boyd was not happy with that. All that morning he had been given a series of conflicting orders. At noon a violent storm had reduced the morale of his troops, who had been under arms for nearly two days. Boyd rode impatiently to the riverbank where he finally received a pencilled order to put his men in motion in twenty minutes, as soon as the guns could be put ashore. That was the last order he got from Wilkinson.

In the battle that followed, Boyd would be in charge of the Americans. He had once been a soldier of fortune, who for twenty years had sold his services to a variety of Indian princes. He exchanged his turban and lance in 1808 for a colonel's commission in the U.S. 4th Infantry. He was a brigadier-general at the opening of the war, but he did not enjoy the trust of his leaders.

Brown couldn't stand him. Scott thought he was an imbecile. Lewis described him as "a combination of ignorance, vanity, and petulance, with nothing to recommend him but that species of bravery in the field which is vaporing, boisterous, stifling reflection, blinding observation." In short, Brigadier-General Boyd was not the best man to put up against highly trained British soldiers.

Boyd's first move was to send in Colonel Eleazar Ripley's regiment across the muddy fields and over a boggy creek bed to probe Morrison's forward skirmishes in the woods on the British left. Ripley advanced half a mile (792 m) when a line of Canadian Voltigeurs suddenly rose from concealment and fired two volleys at his men.

Ignoring the cries of their officers, the Americans leapt behind stumps and began to open individual fire until their ammunition was exhausted. After that they ran back out of British range. Ripley retired with them but soon returned to the attack with reinforcements and drove the Voltigeurs back.

John Sewell, the British lieutenant whose breakfast was so rudely interrupted, was standing with his fellow Green Tigers in the thin line formed by the two British regiments when he saw their grey-clad Voltigeurs burst from the woods on his left, chased by the Americans. The situation was critical. If Ripley's men could get around the 89th, which held the left flank, and attack the British from the rear, the battle was as good as lost.

Morrison now executed the first of a series of parade-ground manoeuvres. The 89th Regiment was facing east. He wheeled them about to face north. As they poured out of the woods, the Americans ran into this solid line of scarlet-coated men, all firing their muskets in unison. That volley of hot lead caused them to break and run.

The contrast between the fire of the opposing forces was so distinct that the women and children hiding in Captain John Crysler's cellar could easily tell the American guns

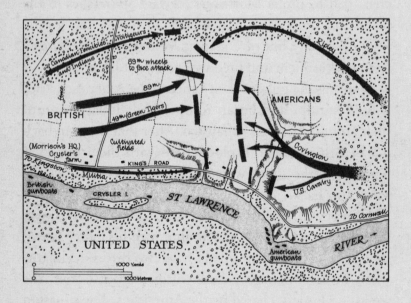

The Battle of Crysler's Farm, Phase I

from the British. The American guns made a steady pop-pop-pop. The latter, at regular intervals, resounded "like a tremendous roll of thunder."

Unable to turn the British left wing, Boyd advanced his three main brigades across the open wheat fields to try to seize the British right wing. A forty-five-year-old Marylander, Leonard Covington, who commanded the 3rd Brigade, was fooled by the grey coats of the 49th right in front of them.

"Come, lads, let me see how you will deal with these militiamen," he shouted. But the disguised Tigers were already executing another drill. They moved in a series

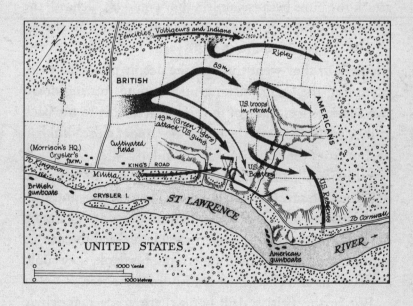

The Battle of Crysler's Farm, Phase II

of staggered platoons each overlapping its neighbour. Supported by six-pounders, the troopers fired rolling volleys against the advancing Americans.

By this time the action was general – a confused mêlée of struggling men, half-obscured by dirty grey smoke, weaving forward and backward, floundering in the ankle-deep mud, splashing and dying in the stream beds, tumbling into gullies, clawing their way out of ravines, until no one, when it was over, was able to produce a coherent account of exactly what had gone on.

By this time the American big guns had been hauled from the boats and were getting into position to harass the advancing British. Morrison ordered the Green Tigers to attack the guns because, unless they could be silenced, the grapeshot would cut the outnumbered British to pieces.

The Tigers were about 120 yards (108 m) from the enemy. Off they went through the deeply ploughed field, trampling the grain, kicking up the mud, tearing down two snake fences that got in their way, unable to fire back as they struggled with the heavy logs under a dreadful hail of shot from the American six-pounders.

John Sewell, advancing with his company into this hail of grapeshot, saw his captain killed. He took over and suddenly spotted a squadron of American dragoons galloping down the King's road on his right. He realized the danger at once. If these horsemen got around his flank, they could circle about and charge the British from the rear.

But in the British drill book there was a manoeuvre

Sewell's company fires on the American dragoons.

specifically arranged to meet this kind of threat. The right wing simply wheeled *backwards* to the left until it faced the line of cavalry. Sewell noted that the entire movement, which the Americans thought was a retreat, was carried out with all the coolness of a parade-ground review as the commands rang out over the crash of grapeshot and canister; *Halt . . . Front . . . Pivot . . . Cover . . . Left wheel into line . . . Fire by platoons from the centre to the flank*. The effect was shattering as the wounded American horses, snorting and neighing, floundered about with their saddles empty.

At the same time, a company of the 89th, stationed well ahead of the main ravine, charged the American guns, captured a six-pounder, and killed its crew. By now the whole American line was crumbling and the retreat was saved from becoming a rout only by the presence of the American reserves. The Battle of Crysler's Farm was over. Again, a small force of British and Canadians had beaten a superior American army.

CHAPTER SEVEN

~

A bitter ending

Major-General James Wilkinson had spent the entire day in his bunk, lamenting his ill fortune at not being with his men. He tried to prevent the pell-mell rush to the boats, exclaiming that the British would say the Americans were running away and claim the victory. He sent a message to Brigadier-General Boyd asking him if he could hold the bank until the night to preserve some vestige of American honour. Boyd's answer was a curt *no*. The men, he said, were exhausted and famished, and they needed a complete night of rest.

Boyd now busied himself with the necessary report of the day's action, which, as always in defeat, was a masterpiece of doubletalk. He couldn't claim victory but he came as close to it as he could, larding his account with a series of alibis. Boyd admitted the result of the action was "not so brilliant and decisive as I could have wished." But he blamed the bad weather, the fatigue of the troops, the lack of sleep, the superiority of the enemy (which was untrue), the superior position of the British, the presence of the gunboats, the surprise, the lack of American guns, and so on.

Wilkinson, however, didn't shilly-shally in his report to the secretary of war. He inflated the British strength from a realistic 800 to 2,170. He bumped up the British casualties from 170 to 500, and said that "although the imperious obligations of duty did not allow me sufficient time to rout the enemy, they were beaten."

But it was Wilkinson who was beaten. "Emaciated almost to a skeleton, unable to sit my horse, or to move ten paces without assistance," he was looking for an excuse to give up the grand campaign. He got it the following morning after the battle in the form of a letter from Major-General Hampton.

The two armies – Hampton's and Wilkinson's – were supposed to meet below the Long Sault, at St. Regis just opposite Cornwall. Wilkinson's flotilla made the passage but Hampton was not there, nor would he ever be.

He wrote that it was impossible to get troops to transport enough supplies to the big river to feed the army. His arrival would only weaken the existing forces and the roads were impractical for wheeled transport. His troops were raw, sick, exhausted, dispirited.

Hampton intended – or so he reported – to go back to Plattsburgh on Lake Champlain and strain every effort to continue the invasion south of Montreal. Actually, he intended to do nothing.

That gave Wilkinson the scapegoat he needed to protect

his own reputation. Montreal was just three days down the river, virtually defenceless. Hampton's sudden withdrawal at Châteauguay had convinced the British high command to withdraw the bulk of British troops to Kingston. Wilkinson still had some seven thousand soldiers. But neither he nor his generals had the will to continue. A hastily summoned council of war agreed to abandon the enterprise.

Wilkinson went to some effort to make it clear that the grand plan was entirely Hampton's fault. In his General Order on November 13, he announced that he was "compelled to retire by the extraordinary unexampled, and apparently unwarrantable conduct of Major-General Hampton."

He wrote to Secretary of War John Armstrong that with Hampton's help he could have taken Montreal in eight or ten days, but now all his hopes were blasted: "I disclaim the shadow of blame because I have done my duty. . . . To General Hampton's outrage of every principle of subordination and discipline may be ascribed the failure of the expedition. . . ."

The American army now drifted eighteen miles (29 km) down the St. Lawrence to Salmon Creek and moved up the tributary to the American hamlet of French Mills, soon to be known as Fort Covington in honour of the dead brigadier-general. Here, in the dreary wilderness of pine and hemlock, with little shelter and hard rations, the Americans passed a dreadful winter.

Sickness, desertions, and greed did more damage than any British force. Clothing was hard to come by. Little Jarvis Hanks, the drummer boy, had no pantaloons and was forced to tailor himself a pair out of one of his two precious blankets. Driven to subsist on polluted bread, the men sickened by the hundreds and died by the score.

So many men died that funeral music was banned from the camp for reasons of morale. By the end of December, almost eighteen hundred were ill. The food was so scarce the sick had to subsist on oatmeal, which was originally ordered for poultices.

All the efficient officers had gone on furlough or were themselves ill with pneumonia, diarrhoea, dysentery, typhoid, or atrophy of the limbs, a kind of dry rot. The remainder, ex-politicians mostly, fattened their pocket-books by selling off army rations to British and Americans alike, and drawing dead men's pay.

The defeat on the St. Lawrence wrecked the careers of the men who bungled the attack. Wilkinson, convalescing in his comfortable home at Malone, New York, and bitterly blaming everybody but himself for the defeat, must have known his days were numbered. Hampton, to the relief of all, would shortly quit the army. Lewis and Boyd had each taken a leave of absence and would never be heard of again.

Along the St. Lawrence, the settlers began to rearrange the fragments of their lives. The north shore had been heavily plundered of cattle, grain, and winter forage.

Fences had been ripped apart to build fires – the sky so lit up that it sometimes seemed as if the entire countryside was ablaze. Cellars, barns, and stables had been looted.

Stragglers, pretending to search for arms, rummaged through houses, broke open trunks, stole everything from ladies' petticoats to men's pantaloons. Fancy china, silver plate, jewellery, books – all these went to the plunderers in spite of Wilkinson's proclamation that private property would be respected.

The Americans left a legacy of bitterness. Dr. William "Tiger" Dunlop, an assistant surgeon with the 89th working with the wounded of both armies in the various farmhouses that did duty as makeshift hospitals, discovered he could not trust some of the Loyalist farmers near the stricken Americans. So great was their hatred of the enemy that they might have killed off the wounded.

Fortunately, this brief explosion in their midst marked the last military excursion down the great river. For John Crysler and his neighbours, the war was over. In spite of James Wilkinson's hollow boast that the attack on Montreal was merely suspended and not abandoned, the St. Lawrence Valley would never again shiver to the crash of alien musketry.

INDEX

Also Available
THE CAPTURE OF DETROIT

Young John Richardson felt as proud as a peacock. At the age of fifteen, a "gentleman volunteer" in the 41st Regiment, he was about to take part in the first Canadian victory in the War of 1812. The British and Canadians were marching on the American fort of Detroit, directly across the river from John's home town of Amherstburg in what is now Ontario. Up ahead he could see the general, Isaac Brock, resplendent in scarlet jacket and gold epaulettes. To the right, flitting through the trees were hundreds of painted warriors under the leadership of the great Shawnee war chief, Tecumseh. The Americans, who had expected to seize Upper Canada without a struggle, were in retreat, holed up within the walls of the Fort. Their own ageing general, William Hull, was hesitant and timorous, fearful of the British cannon balls tearing into his stronghold.

Using the techniques that have made him the country's best-known storyteller, Pierre Berton recreates the dramatic scenes at the start of a war that helped shape the new Canada and define the Canadian character.

THE DEATH OF ISAAC BROCK

Pierre Berton continues the story of the War of 1812 with his graphic description of the most significant battle in Canadian history: the British-Canadian victory at Queenston Heights.

How a small force of regular soldiers, volunteers, and Mohawk Indians trapped and defeated a much larger American army and saved Upper Canada from becoming part of the United States.

And how the nation's greatest general, dashing up the heights above the Niagara River, died bravely but incautiously, thus creating an imperishable legend.

REVENGE OF THE TRIBES

Robert Richardson was just fourteen in the autumn of 1812, a midshipman in the provincial marine. His father, an army surgeon, ordered him to stay out of trouble – for there was certainly trouble enough on the border where the Detroit river flows. But young Richardson could not bear to be out of action. When the British and Indians attacked the Americans at Frenchtown, he was in the thick of one of the bloodiest battles of the war. For it was here, on the banks of the River Raisin, that the Indians exacted a terrible revenge against their American enemies. They had not forgotten the Battle of Tippecanoe the previous year, when a future U.S. president, William Henry Harrison, attacked and destroyed their village on the Wabash. That single event brought the Indians over to the British side to fight under the great Shawnee war chief, Tecumseh.

In this lively account of these two battles, Pierre Berton tells the fascinating story of how the Indians helped prevent another invasion of Canada.

CANADA UNDER SIEGE

The Americans seize Little York (Toronto) and burn the Parliament Buildings.

A young boy leads the Canadians to win the Battle of Stoney Creek.

Laura Secord warns the British of the Battle of Beaver Dams.

James FitzGibbon's "Bloody Boys" hit Black Rock.

Stories of traitors, heroes, guerilla fighters, turncoats, villains, and doomed generals written in Pierre Berton's lively prose make history come alive.

The Battle of Lake Erie

Pierre Berton continues his series on the battles of the War of 1812 in this thrilling saga of men, muskets, cannons, and sailing ships. The great naval battle on Lake Erie in the summer of 1813 was fought by fifteen battleships – nine American, six British – each one of which had been constructed of timber felled on the shores of the lake. In *The Battle of Lake Erie*, Pierre Berton vividly illustrates how two brilliant commanders fought each other to a standstill – and how one turned crushing defeat into a dazzling victory.

The Death of Tecumseh

The Shawnee chief Tecumseh was perhaps the greatest native leader in the War of 1812. Allied with the British, he was both feared and admired by his American foes. In September 1813 in what is now southwestern Ontario, he fought to the death at the Battle of the Thames. To this day, no one has been able to locate Tecumseh's grave, and both his death and life have become the stuff of legend.

Don't Miss

STEEL ACROSS THE SHIELD

The Canadian Shield splits Canada in two. A 1,500-kilometre barrier of rock and muskeg, it hampered settlers of the nineteenth century from having easy access to the fertile plains, rolling hills, and majestic mountains of western Canada. Hampered them, that is, until the mid-1880s when a railway was finally constructed across the Shield to Winnipeg, Manitoba.

Steel Across the Shield is the gripping story of how that railroad line was blasted from ancient rock and floated over vast swamps to connect with the ribbon of steel already being driven across the plains and over the mountains of Alberta and British Columbia. It's also the story of how this transcontinental railway was saved from seeming collapse at the very last moment by an armed rebellion in what is now the province of Saskatchewan.

Steel Across the Shield is another vivid instalment in Pierre Berton's informative, accessible series about the construction of the CPR and the settling of the Canadian West.